Unburying My Identity

The Process of Finding Yourself Through
The Fog of Trauma

Robin Phillips

BookLeaf Publishing

India | USA | UK

Made with ❤ on the BookLeaf Publishing Platform
www.bookleafpub.in
www.bookleafpub.com

Dedication

The dedications in this book are for some very special people. Unfortunately, a few of which will not be able to read it. But I will thank them anyway.

The first dedication I have is for my partner, Shane Bukovskey.
I truly cannot express all you have done for me and all you have helped me with, but I'm going to try.
Thank you for being you.
Thank you for being constant and steadfast in who you are. Thank you for showing me what it is to be someone who is sure of who they are.
I am constantly amazed and grateful at how kind and generous and supportive you are. I have such a respect and admiration for who you are as a person. Thank you for being who I didn't know I needed when I needed you the most. Thank you for showing me that silence isn't something to fear and that sometimes, people truly are who they say they are. You have been, and continue to be, a shining example of how to respect and care for yourself; while doing that, you also care for me too. Your effort and consideration and love do not go unnoticed. The respect and consideration you show me in all situations is incredible and I am a very lucky person to

have found you.

Thank you for helping me find who I am again and for not giving up on the person I was.

You are an incredible human being, and I look forward to continuing to be amazed by you for many, many years to come. I love you. <3

The next dedication is in memory of my great aunt, Rose Williams.

Rosie, thank you for being so supportive of me writing a second book. Thank you for being who you were and thank you for the opportunities we had to watch frogs in their makeshift ponds, watch your favorite shows, and talk about every subject we could think of. Thank you for all of our talks and puzzle pieces. I love you and miss you. Say hi to Uncle Danny for us down here.

The third is in memory of my aunt Coleen Walsh. Auntie, you were a rockstar. Not in the actual up on the stage sense, but in every other sense of the words. I will cherish every memory I have of us, every Rennaissance Faire I wear your handmade costume to, and every line of "Somewhere Over the Rainbow", every time I hear it. I wish you were still here to read this book. I know you would be so excited. Thank you for being who you were. I love you and miss you.

Preface

For many people, therapy consists of an office and a therapist.
For me, therapy comes in the form of writing.

Many of the writings in this book were written during panic attacks, moments of anger, frustration, and sadness.
I know I am not alone in these emotions or problems. I know you have likely been there too.

If you can relate to the writings in this book, I hope they help you feel less alone in this world. I hope they show you that progress is possible, but it takes a hell of a lot of work to get there. It is not easy to do, but I believe in you.

If you can't relate to these writings, I hope they can help you learn what these things are like. In learning about others' experiences and how those experiences affect them, we learn about ourselves as well.

Lastly, for anyone reading this who is looking for a reason to stay, this is it. <3
I know it is difficult to be in the world when you don't

even feel human. I know it can feel impossible to make any progress at all. I am proud of you for trying.

One step at a time, one day at a time.

You are not alone. There is always someone who cares.

<3

-National Suicide Prevention Helpline: 1 (800) 273-TALK or 988

-National Domestic Violence Hotline: 1 (800) 799-SAFE or text "LOVEIS" to 22522

-Substance Abuse & Mental Health Services Helpline: 1 (800) 662-HELP

-National Alliance for Eating Disorders Helpline: 1 (866) 662-1235

-(RAINN) Rape Abuse and Incest National Network: 1 (800) 656-HOPE

-LGBT National Hotline: 1 (888) 843-4564

-The Trevor Project: 1 (866) 488-7386

-(NAMI) National Alliance on Mental Illness: 1 (800) 950-6264

Acknowledgements

To those who have loved and supported me through this life, in any stage of it, thank you. You have all helped shape who I am.

To those who have hurt me, some in ways that I am still healing from, you were part of my story, but you won't determine my future.

To those I have hurt during my life, I am so sorry. I have not always been the person who picks others up when they are down. I have been the antagonist in many stories. I am truly sorry for being any negative part of your story.

I am determined to spend whatever time I have trying to improve myself and the world around me, however possible.

To the person reading this book, thank you for being here. I appreciate you.

1. The Daily Effects of Disabilities

If all you do is survive today, it is okay.

If all you can do today is breathe and wait for the sun to set again, it is okay.

If all the responsibilities you have need to wait until you can lift yourself from the covers, they will be there when you get up.

If you can't get up quickly, but must first sit, then stand to keep from falling, that's okay.

If you don't have any idea who to be or where to be right now, that's okay.

If you aren't where you thought you would be at 21, 30, 45, it is okay to be at a different destination than you started walking towards.

If your pain makes you want to cry and sit in one place while the day happens, you are not a bad person for doing that.

And if people call you lazy, unmotivated, or don't see the effort you are putting in just to be awake, don't worry about it.

They don't see the effort because they don't see your struggle.

I do.

I am the struggle some days in similar ways.

I too wince when sitting up in bed, and then again when standing up.

I too have days where putting pants or socks on is one of my biggest physical challenges.

I too have days where I would rather stay in bed and cry from the pain than go to work.

I too have days where I wonder why I must deal with my body rebelling against me all the time.

I too see the confusion in the looks when I suddenly wince or sharply inhale because changing positions while standing caused my joints to lose their hold and resolve.

I too feel the pain that is surviving.

I too want it to end.

Anyone with chronic pain knows this story. People with mental health conditions as well.

I know this story all too well.

I know the parts of the story that no one sees. I know the parts that no one wants to see or be made aware of.

Some people don't know how to act around us. As if we were some odd species that they just can't understand.

We are all people.

The difference between perception and reality though is who is seeing it.

My perception of my disabilities and mental health

struggles are much different than yours.

Guess what?

That is okay.

You don't have to come into the conversation knowing all of the answers. I don't expect you to know why I wince or why sometimes, I need to sit down, lean against a wall, or hop to a chair without warning.

I know you don't understand. That is okay.

But please, don't allow your lack of knowledge to come out of your mouth in the form of judgement or ridicule.

We don't want this life.

We don't want the constant pain, the overthinking, dizziness, the fear of it only getting worse and never any better.

I don't want my disabilities. But I have them.

Some people think that stating I have disabilities is for pity, extra help, sympathy, or just to complain. It isn't.

I talk about my disabilities to help raise awareness.

What you say and do affects people.

The looks you give someone who is already unable to stand because they are leaning on the shelf you need aren't helping. The looks you give when you say "but you don't look sick" just add to the ignorance of the comment.

I know I don't look sick. I know I look as though I can take on mountains. I know I seem like the world is at my will and not the other way around.
I do this on purpose. Because whenever I have been open about being disabled or having mental health struggles, I've been pitied or underestimated.
Having people assume I can't do something without even asking if I can, that's a shitty feeling.
Disabilities don't necessarily mean I am always unable. It means that I have limits, they are different every day, so I will be differently abled <u>every day</u>.

On the days where I seem like I can do anything, there is still pain there. It never completely goes away. Some days are better than others. None are pain-free. I can just tolerate it better now.

Don't treat me like I don't have worth because of my disabilities.

IF you do, I will not feel worthless because of your comments, but I will recognize that it is worthless to have you around.

I am of as much worth as I feel I am, and I am worth my weight in gold for what I put up with and live through every day.

2. I Wish I Would Have Known

I wish I would have known why life was so hard, so much more difficult than other people made it seem.
I wish I would have known that me being a kid with big emotions and even bigger fears wasn't odd or misplaced or weird. It is the life of someone with emotional dysregulation.
I wish I would have known that my talking and conversational intrusions weren't just me being annoying or obnoxious. It was me not knowing what impulsivity was or that I was the definition of it.

I wish that I'd known that other people's opinions of me and who I am weren't more important than mine, that I didn't have to be the way people told me I needed to be. That I could just be myself and the right people would love me anyway.
But the torment that was name calling, teasing, poking and prodding, and mentions of my body type and how much I ate weren't harmless as others thought. They could have been, had I been able to understand that the opinions of others didn't have to mean anything to me. But I grew up knowing only the opinions of others. My opinion seemed to mean nothing to anyone else, they

didn't take me seriously, so why was I supposed to believe that my opinion was supposed to mean something to me? If everyone around you comments on only the things they would like you to change, how are you supposed to know there is anything to keep the same? If you are told you talk too much or are too loud every time you open your mouth, how are you supposed to want to talk at all? The combination of having so much to say but no one who will truly hear you within your household, what are you supposed to do? What was I supposed to do?

So, I tried to be who they wanted. I tried to be exactly as I should and I tried to correct everything they didn't like. They didn't like how much or how loud or how fast I talked, so I slowed down, quieted down, tamped myself down, until all that was left was relevant information that I knew would still likely go unheard and misunderstood.
They didn't like how annoying I was, so I spent less time around them in hopes that the lack of time would lead to a lack of annoyance. It didn't though. The times I was around just got shorter as I realized that I could not will the annoyance away for them. The only way to take the annoyance away was to take myself away.

I realized in time that I couldn't fix every issue they had

with me because in doing so, I would no longer be me. Maybe that's what they wanted. For a while, I tried to give them that. I tried to be the person they wanted on the outside, keeping myself safe inside my head, being who I was around the people who truly valued me as myself.

I had to hide who I was from everyone, not because their comments meant they hated me, but because the comments made me hate myself. As someone who weighed everyone's opinions of me over my own, I started to hate myself because I could never be who they wanted me to be. I could never actually fully be the quieter, calmer, less eccentric person they wanted me to be on the inside, I could only manifest it on the outside.

So, I did as much as I could. When I was around the people who preferred me to be that quieter, calmer, more normal person, I pretended I was. I pretended to not have as many thoughts, pretended to not care where we went to eat, what people did, what they said. I pretended so hard that the person inside of me started to wilt. I started to crumble inside. I started to die inside, a little more with each passing comment or glance. But they loved it. They loved me. And they actually seemed to like me, which I had never seen them do before. Except they didn't like me. They liked the mask of neutrality that I had created for them to see. I started out only wearing it for them. Just at home. Then I wore it more and more until it was my constant reality around anyone who wasn't me. While my exterior got stronger and tougher, the child inside of me died. I buried her in a shallow grave, shallow at first at the hope that she would have her moment. Then deeper still, every time a comment was made, an opinion told, a new person feeling the same about that grave-bound girl that everyone else did. Every hole that was pierced in my soul sent that girl deeper into the ground. The grave wasn't shallow anymore.

Masking became a reality for me, much too young. I learned that instead of trying to get the people who loved me to like me for who I was, I could get them to like what I did and who I tried to be. And that's what I have done my whole life. I've pretended to be one person for those who make it clear that they don't like me for who I actually am. They think they see me for me when I am actually truly another person all together.

For the longest time, I pretended to be the person everyone liked. I mirrored others' actions and phrasings; I did the things people told me they liked and pretended to dislike things I loved so I could be loved instead. What I can tell you over everything else, it wasn't worth it. As much as losing people who are supposed to like you for who you are sucks, losing yourself is so much worse. Losing yourself and then deciding that you liked who you were all along is devastating. Because now you have a choice to make and a question to answer.

Do I like the girl in the not so shallow grave enough to dig her back out? And am I willing to do the work to get back to her? I chose yes to both.
Retrieving yourself from the hole you dug is frustrating. It is even more frustrating to look back at your entire life and realize that if you had just known the things you know now, if someone had just told you that being who you actually are is what you need to do to find your people, you never would have buried her. You never would have dug to begin with. The act of burying and unburying the parts of you that no one else could ever seem to stand is so emotionally draining.
If I would have just known that people aren't the ones who determine my worth, maybe I wouldn't have grown up feeling worthless whenever I wasn't actively helping someone.
If I would have just known that not everyone who is in your life is supposed to be there or stay there, I could've learned to let go of the people trying to change me instead of turning into one of them. If I had known how offensive and detrimental the things I did as that person were, I never would have done them.

If I had just known, I would've been me instead of her. I would've improved and worked on me instead of trying to work on everything and everyone else. Instead of putting on a mask that slowly suffocated who I really was, I could have breathed the same air everyone else breathed and felt like I deserved to be alive as they were.
The thing is, I didn't know though.

I wish I would have known. I could have saved her. Now I must learn to save myself.

3. "Just Do..." Doesn't Work

She looked at the dishes in the sink and sighed.

How do people do this every day?
Clean their dishes, fold their clothes, shower, or any of
the countless things that were piling up around her. How
did everyone get those things done?

Didn't they deal with fatigue so strong that you wake up
from a nap needing another? Did they not see that pile
of clothes as a mountain to climb, rather than the
molehill it is?
Are there some people out there that can do their dishes
every day, eat three meals, shower, do all their hygiene
tasks, and still have enough energy and motivation to do
anything else?
Why doesn't she get to be one of those people? She
wants to know what doing your laundry daily is like.
Doing tasks as they come up and not falling behind and
then into the abyss, farther than before.
She wants desperately to know how motivation feels
when it sticks around. Hers always runs off, like an
untrained dog on a scent, never coming back, even when
you beg. She wanted to know what she could do without
the brain fog, exhaustion, and lack of motivation

constantly bursting into her nicely planned day and tearing up her to-do list.

She wanted to do what others did so easily. But depression likes to tear up your lists, erase your energy, and make that mountain of laundry feel like the biggest climb of your life.

So, climb you do.

4. Am I Annoying or Are You Just Annoyed?

"You're so annoying, you should talk less, can't get a
word in edgewise."
I'm not annoying.
You are annoyed.
There is a difference.

Why does me being me cause you so much angst?
Why is it that me talking and wanting to share
information with you is such a grievance?
Why do you complain about how much I talk then ask if
I'm okay when I don't?
Why?

You are annoyed.
You being annoyed stems from something inside you,
not from me.
I am being myself.
Whatever reason you have for disliking and being
annoyed by those parts of me that I choose to show you,
that is a reason that is yours to deduce.
It is yours to figure out and yours to fix.
That burden should never have been placed on me.
The burden of your anxiety and your overwhelming

feelings and your dislike should never have been made my problem.

How dare you try to stifle the person I was to benefit yourself.
How dare you make me believe that I couldn't exist as myself.
How dare you not notice when I was trying to show you that the things you were doing and saying hurt me.

That burden never should have been mine.
Just like you ignoring my feelings and emotions, dismissing them like idle woes when they were really cries for help.
The kind you only hear a few times before the person stops crying out.
Then they cry in instead.
Inside themselves and their minds.
Inside their own walls.
In their solitude.

When the person has cried out for help in the only ways they know how without actually saying "help", which always seemed like a daunting and defeating task in a word, has found none, they stop crying out.
They start trying to find ways to cope. Ways to deal with what is going on inside their heads. Inside their bodies.

Inside their souls.

I looked for help. Then I cried in.
I cried within myself and found ways that helped me
through. Not healthy ways, but ways.
Self-harm's description is in the name, but unless you've
been in the deepest darkest place where self-harm seems
the only way to mediate the emotions and spinning
thoughts inside your head, the name is all you see. You
see someone who has lost control and needs your help.
You aren't wrong at that moment.

Here's the thing though.

That person needed your help long before you saw those
cuts. And the person who self-harms in ways you've
never seen, they need your help too. The ones who will
never have scars, never use a blade, or break skin, the
ones who chose routes that are less likely to be
discovered, they need your help too.

Your perfectionist, super helpful, self-reliant, "wise for
their age" people need your help too.

Before they ever get to the point of feeling so alone in
their life that sitting in their room, tugging their own
hair out of their head seems to be the best way they can

find to keep the storm inside of them from destroying them. They don't know how to control that storm yet. They don't know what the storm is even capable of.

They need help.
Before self-harm even becomes an option.

Mixing thoughts and swirling emotions and outside voices and opinions don't make a very good combination to take in while trying to figure out who you are.
Being told how annoying you are, even with no ill intent, can alter your view of yourself.
Hearing someone you look up to insult someone's weight makes you wonder if they'll feel the same about you if you ever get bigger than they see fit. Hearing people talk over you or not even enter your opinion into the discussion makes you start to be distrustful of yourself.

If no one else wants to hear my opinion, why do I have one?

When you are a young child, trying to watch those around you and try to figure out who to be, so many small moments can skew your vision of things.
Comments not even directed at you can change the way you live your life, add a new anxiety, or change the way

you see someone.

I'm not annoying.
You are annoyed.
That burden is yours to carry.
It never should have been mine.
And it never will be again.

5. Must Be Nice

"Must be nice to be skinny."
"You are so small."
"You're so tiny."

Must be nice?
Must be fucking nice?

No, it's not. It is fucking rough. Do you know why I'm skinny? Have you thought about why? Or are you just seeing me for the exterior and assuming I'm trying to do this to myself?
Take a minute and think about the reasons I could be skinny and the reasons you shouldn't mention it unless I do. The reasons I could be skinny. The reasons I am. I have chronic pain and food issues and blood sugar issues. Hypoglycemia wrecks my day, but my inability to eat sometimes makes it so much worse. I'm either binge eating, too nauseous to eat, or I forget to eat all together. For anyone about to think that I should "just be better" about my eating habits should work on their judgement and perception. Don't you think that I would've fixed my eating habits already if it was that fucking easy?

Now for the reasons you shouldn't bring it up every

chance you get. Or at all really unless I'm talking about it.

The number one reason is that every single time I look in the mirror, I know why I look like this.

I know I'm small, tiny, skinny, thin. I know that it is the goal for a lot of people. While I can appreciate how I look right now, I would rather be a bit heavier if it meant I could eat. Every time my weight is mentioned, it just reminds me of my struggles with food and weight. It reminds me that my body dysmorphia is only temporarily silent because my eating habits are so bad. My body dysmorphia loves when I am skinny, but I'd rather have body dysmorphia than intermittent nausea, extreme hunger, and food sensory issues. I'd rather be heavy than sick and fucking tired.

I know people that bring it up probably think that they aren't causing any harm. I don't normally say anything because people get defensive when they realize they've unintentionally upset someone. But here is a PSA for everyone who wants to mention anything about someone's body.

Just a few things to consider before opening your mouth. 1) Is what you want to say a compliment, a backwards comment, or a criticism? If it is anything but the first, keep it to yourself.

2) Is the comment appropriate? If not, keep it to yourself.
3) If you feel you need to correct something about someone's exterior appearance, remind yourself that if it isn't something they can fix within 5 minutes of you mentioning it, just don't.

Don't tell someone their shirt is ugly because they can't just change. If someone had a piece of lint on them or something in their teeth or toilet paper stuck to their shoe, by all means, say something. Don't just ruin someone's day or make them feel shitty about what they look like just because you decided to open your mouth and offer an unsolicited comment.

You don't know why that person is the size they are and you have no idea what they may go through on a daily basis because of that.
Someone who is skinny could have an eating disorder, a nutrition deficiency, a chronic health condition, or many other things.
Someone who is bigger could have PCOS, a thyroid condition, an eating disorder, or anything else.

If we want your opinion on how we look, we will tell you.
Feel free to compliment us on the things we choose! The clothes we picked out, the hair color we chose, makeup,

jewelry, shoes, nails, tattoos, etc. If you feel that you must compliment or comment on anything physical, please choose something we chose.

It will make all the difference.

6. Unsolicited Advice

Just because I told you my story doesn't give you all
expenses paid rights to tell me what will help.
Not what I should do or try, what I should eat or take,
how I should feel, or what pain management I should
use.
Please don't bother telling me who I should be, what I
should use, where I should go, how I should react, or
what will help me.

I've been living in this body for my whole life. I spent a
lot of my life in pain no one could explain, so instead
they called me a hypochondriac or said I'm too dramatic.
No one could offer any helpful responses, so instead they
offer useless ones. Try this, eat that, take this, do that, go
here, don't go there, don't do that, the list goes on and
on.

How about we compromise? If you tell me I should go to
a certain doctor, I will get to tell you where to buy your
clothes. If you tell me to use pills instead of cannabis for
pain, I get to tell you what food you can eat for dinner. If
you give me advice on something that you don't
experience, I get to give you equally useless information
about how unhealthy your diet is or how your clothes

could fit better if you just tried.

Everyone is out here thinking they know best when they don't even know me or my pain. Other people have it worse, someone always has it worse. Just because someone has it worse doesn't mean what I deal with isn't bad. It doesn't mean that I shouldn't express how I feel about it. It doesn't mean I don't get to have a bad day. Or multiple bad days. Sometimes, for a stretch, every day is a bad day. For my pain, for my mental health, for anything that I deal with.

Stop giving me advice on something that you wouldn't know existed if I didn't vocalize it.
I'm not telling you so you feel bad for me, or you solve my problems, or you offer me a half-cocked "fix" that may or may not work. If I wanted those things, I would ask for them. But I don't. I didn't tell you what's wrong so you could attempt to humpty dumpty me back together again. I told you either because you asked or because I wanted you to know for some reason.

Please don't make me regret telling you what's going on inside of me by pretending that you know better about it. Your ten minutes of hearing me describe my issues doesn't qualify you to tell me what to do or try or fix. It only qualifies you to listen. If you can't listen without suggestions, please let me know so I can stop telling you things.

If you told someone of your issues to help them understand what is wrong and instead of offering an ear and support, they offered you multiple suggestions and then got upset when you told them that their suggestions aren't helpful, how would you feel? Would you feel like they are listening to understand or listening to respond? Which would you want?

7. Why Is This My Life?

Why is this my life?

Why the ankle brace, the dislocations, the random pains and muscle twitches?

Why is this how I live? Why is it how I will die?

Anxious, in pain, dizzy, unable to amble my way across the floor because my body decided its parts didn't want to stay where they were meant to be. Not what was needed to top off the months of almost constant anxiety from outside sources.

Why does pain and anguish have to be my baseline state?
Why is there never a day that I am allowed to wake up in peace?

Even on the very few days a year I wake up without an immediate onslaught of pain, the insomnia has done me in, or my mind is alive with the sound of chaos before my eyes click open for the first time. I've already considered how this day could go wrong before I've opened my eyes to see if the day has indeed begun again.

I keep them shut, hoping this will be the day when the world stays dark and quiet.

The days where no pain is immediately present, the abyss of exhaustion and the pit of anxiety have already begun convincing me that I don't need to drive to work today. They are convincing me that I don't have to be a main character in my life.

The days where those thoughts beat the physical pain to the punch can sometimes be worse than the days that my body feels like it is being torn apart. But I smile and grit my teeth and go about my life trying to make sure that other people are having a better time than me. Some people can't be helped, but I am there for those who can.

No one should have to feel this way.

8. Social Anxiety and the Fear of Being Perceived

Are they looking at me? Why are they whispering? Why do so many people have to be shopping today?

She shuffles a million already answered questions through her head as a veiled attempt at surviving her grocery trip. Every person is an obstacle, every conversation a chore, every passing minute making her want to leave her cart in the aisle and go get some air. She felt like she was suffocating and weighed the options.

She needed food for her fridge because of the last two planned grocery trips she had 'postponed' already that week. So, she took a deep breath, kept her head down, and tried to get the last few items she needed to fill her all too empty fridge.

Hard to have food when you don't go buy any.

Some days, the mere thought of walking into a grocery store causes more anxiety than the drive there. She moves her cart to the side, attempting to take up as little room as possible. She scans her list and goes to find a register. Once the anxiety of payment methods is over and she has waited awkwardly for the bagger, she leaves the store and the anxiety behind.

She let go of the breath she didn't know she was holding
and unclenched her shoulders for the first time since she
walked through the doors.

9. Dishes Aren't Just Dishes

She starts the dishes before relaxing for the night. She soaps up a plate and puts it onto another in the sink, waiting to be rinsed off. The plates clinked together as they met, a short-lived sound to anyone but her.

She used to apologize for that. She used to apologize for the sound of the dishes clanking "too loud". When she was responsible for interrupting his show or game with that "noise".
He sighed in the other room, shooting her a look that he didn't care if she saw.

She knew all the words he wasn't saying with that sigh. She had heard the words before. Those words were written in what was left of her soul at one point. She didn't need him to say the words to feel the judgment and pointed stares. She knew that the sound annoyed him.

He didn't always just sigh and look pointedly at her before turning back to the tv. He used to use those words. She didn't need to hear them again because she had heard them too many times to count. Until just giving her a look could tell her all the words he wanted to say in no time at all.

Why are you being so loud?
I can't believe you. Are you trying to wake the whole
house up? You are so inconsiderate. Maybe think of
someone else for once in your life.
Or comments about being useless because if you can't do
it silently to appease the others, why do it at all? But she
can't answer the question he didn't tell her was
rhetorical. She either did them and got his reaction,
however harsh it may be, or she dealt with his mother
and father in the morning. She always made the choice
every night as to whose wrath to incur and rolled with
the punches. No matter what, she was screwed. So, it
was a game of who is in a better mood tonight vs who is
pissed in the morning and looking for someone to take it
out on. She wasn't technically family, so apparently she
was fair game. That's how they acted. No one held
anyone accountable, everyone was in the cycle of abuse.

The problem was, she did think about everyone else. It
was impossible not to when she was always watching
her back. When she knew that every decision she made
wasn't good enough. That nothing she was going to be
able to do would be good enough. And every reaction
from them was a game of Russian roulette. She never
knew who was going to be angry, at who, about what.

And somehow, they managed to blame her for things she knew she didn't do but she can't just defend yourself. It is 3 against 1. Are you crazy?

So, what options are there?
Correct them and see how many of them spew hatred toward you, calling you a liar and telling you that they don't believe you? Agree to what they are saying and incur the punishment for whatever they deemed your role was in the drama? Often it was that their feud wouldn't have happened if she hadn't made one of them angry first. She never knew she was involved until the fights began, so she just chose the lesser of the two evils she was presented with and took the assigned punishment.

She tried not to think about the forms of punishment they liked. Her brain had blocked most of it out. Her brain used to make her relive them, so she tried not to subject herself to torture if not for a good cause. The fights happened a lot and they were over small things that seemed huge to her at the time because of the problems they brought. One of their favorites was the dishes.

10. PTSD in the Weirdest of Places

Why does my brain hate me so much?

Why does it hold onto all of the bad things and bring them up like they are trying to "show me my card". This isn't a magic show, and I don't want to be on this ride. I didn't want to be on the ride that caused all of this either; but here I am.

Here I am dealing with the anxiety and the tears, the anger and the feeling of helplessness that I only feel when this happens.

I don't have flashbacks anymore but that doesn't mean I don't have PTSD. I'm not cured because I don't see him in my dreams or have him invading my brain and taking me back there again and again. It is still PTSD even when that part finally, mercifully, stops and you are left to work on the NEXT part of your "healing journey". When is the journey over? When does it STOP? Please make it stop..

It has been so many years, and I can still remember how I felt in those moments. I still know what it felt like, what he said to me, although his voice finally faded a few years back.

How much healing have I done since I left? So much.
More than I ever thought I would be alive to do. I have
lived more days than I ever imagined having. Than I ever
planned on having. Than I thought I was allowed to
have. It's so overwhelming to still be alive so many years
after you thought you would die. After you wanted to
die. After you almost pulled the trigger.
But I didn't. And I'm here.

I don't know how I am still here. Between depression,
near death experiences, suicidal ideation, domestic
violence, temporary homelessness, and all the other
things, how am I still here? And why? Please tell me
why I am still enduring this. Please tell me why I can still
see him in my friends when they yell and wave their
hands, hear the same kind of anger in a man's voice at
the grocery store and freeze, my body not knowing what
to do because I don't know what to do because my brain
doesn't seem to realize we aren't there anymore.

WE AREN'T THERE ANYMORE BRAIN! WHY WON'T
YOU LISTEN?

Why won't you leave me alone?
Do I have to do this forever?
Does it have to take so long?
I'm putting in the work and I'm getting results and then

all of a sudden, a wave of hands and raising of voices
means that I don't have control of myself anymore.
Do you know how scary that is? Do you know how
badly I want to be able to tell someone what's going on
in those moments? Do you know how badly I want to
not have those moments? I'm out but I'm not. I'm out
and I'm safe but my mind isn't safe.

I'm physically safe but my mind is a prison, the bars
clear as glass so I can see a world outside of those bars
but reaching it seems impossible but looks so close. It
looks so close and I feel I can touch it and then I hit the
bars so violently from running so fast that I almost make
myself bleed. I reach past those bars and when I can't
reach farther, I stare at the outside world with abandon,
wondering if I'll ever be out there. Can someone like me
be out there? Ever? Or am I too broken, like that toy
with the broken wheel that isn't broken enough to throw
away but not nice enough where you can use it for any
real purpose. Can I be out there? Or is that not in the
cards for me? Every time I stare too long out those bars
and imagine too hard that I'm out there, beyond the bars,
the trauma that floods back and something always
reminds me of where I am.

11. When The Mind and Body Can't Agree

My mind and body can't agree.
My mind knows I'm safe, but my body is positive I'm not. Shaking, crying, rocking. Wishing my brain could overrule my body this time too. Hear anger, feel like you're in danger. The body's pattern, again and again. Until everything seems scary. Even someone my brain knows would never hurt me.

My body doesn't care what my brain thinks. My body senses danger. It senses fear and fear brings up old memories, some that I wish I could forget. I try to remind my body; they are different though. They are not the same. One was callous and cruel and took pleasure from my pain while the other is kind and gentle and would never choose to harm me.

My body doesn't believe it. Even as I think of the word harm in this state, the tears well up yet again with thoughts of the person who wasn't so kind. The person who derived so much happiness from my despair, from my pain. My body remembers that. It thinks we are back there again, but we aren't. How do I convince it? How do I convince my body we are safe? Finally, definitely, completely safe with this person.

How do I get my body to stop worrying? How do I tell it that the fight is over. How do I get this to stop happening. The trembling and clenching muscles and held breath and shudders when a noise is heard near the door to the room I hid in a corner in. How do I make my body believe my brain because right now my body wants me to run outside as far as I can while simultaneously hiding in this corner for the rest of my life, never having to face the source of the anger. Never having to worry about being where it gets taken out.

Never realizing the whole time that I don't need to do either. He isn't going to hurt me. He isn't and wouldn't. He isn't going to scream at me or grab me or get in my face. He isn't going to call me names or make me do things to pay him back for making his anger worse. Pay him back for the trouble I cause him seemingly by simply existing.

He isn't going to hurt me. My brain knows that. That is all I'm chanting to my body, all I'm thinking about, all I'm telling myself. Why doesn't my body believe me? Why am I still in this corner, curled up with my knees to my chest, sobbing? Why is it still like this? The memories don't invade my sleep anymore so why do they still invade my body?

How is this problem not gone? Is it ever going to go away? Will this ever stop being my reaction to anger? Will I ever be better? Will I ever be healed? Will my body and my brain ever be able to agree and coexist? I sure hope so because this feeling is as close to hell as I can get, especially when my brain doesn't feel it too.

The panic feels so real, so current, so new. But it is actually old. Dredged up from the back of my mind, pulled up from the deepest depths and forced into every physical cell I have. Havoc is instantaneous and brutal. Chaos and panic combine until my whole body tightens and I feel the effects of a frightened body and a calm mind. I repeat over and over again that he won't hurt me. That he isn't him. That I'm not there anymore.

My brain knows. My body is still learning what safe means in these moments. Safety in anger is an unusual concept for my body to accept, as if written in a language that doesn't work with its binary code.

Hopefully my body learns one day that there can be safety in anger. The two can coexist if given the right host.

12. Writing Down A Breakdown

She is so tired of being disabled.

She knows all the normal responses. "You're lucky to be able to -blah blah blah". No, she's not.

Lucky would be not waking up in pain every day. Lucky wouldn't be frustrated. All the time. At herself. Lucky wouldn't wonder if this is going to be the rest of her life.

Will it get worse? Will there ever be anything that helps? Is this her eternity? Stuck in this body that hates her and not having any choice but to persevere? To progress? To try to make things better for others so they don't feel like she does while also trying to show people that disability has a face?

She is tired. She is so tired of being disabled.
The frustration of not being able to do what she should be able to do, what other people could do, what she could do yesterday.
The frustration of feeling like a disappointment and feeling ashamed because how is she supposed to explain

that she did it yesterday, but she can't do it today and
she isn't yet sure about tomorrow?
How is she supposed to explain that to someone who
doesn't experience it?
How does she explain that her muscles and bones ache
in the morning and just getting to work can require a
moment of stillness before proceeding on with her day.
How does she explain that her body hurts so much that
it feels like hot brands are being pressed to her muscles?
That burning sensation dulling, but lasting a while. 2
days so far.
How does she explain that she is at her limit without
seeming or sounding incapable?
How does she know how he will react? How anyone
will?

And yet, she has to say something. She has to advocate
for herself and know her limits. She needs to reinforce
her limits. She needs to stand up for herself. But she is so
tired of having to stand up for herself. Of having
something to stand up for herself for.

Why did everyone feel owed an explanation or proof
before they believed her pain?
Why was everyone so quick to tell her that she couldn't
be in that much pain because she looked fine? She was
always in pain. That's how it was.

But on nights like that one, she let herself grieve all of the things she couldn't do. She let herself feel the emotions she bottled up every day and hid behind her mask of neutrality. She allowed herself to grieve the parts of her she had to leave behind over the years and the parts of her story that she was nervous to share with others. She let herself grieve the things that being disabled takes from you.

Everyone likes to try to see the silver lining in her story, as if it will make her feel better about being in pain. She knows they mean well, but it is so hard to be called resilient when she has no choice. It is hard to wake up every day and have responsibilities when her body starts screaming before she even opens her eyes.

When standing makes her dizzy and she has to put test weight on her ankles to make sure they are both in their sockets. If one isn't, it is a brace day. The brace is uncomfortable but she works with it. She has to tie it tightly to keep her haphazard ankle in place while she runs through the day's chores and workload. The brace keeps the ankle in, but it doesn't take away the pain, as well as the ankle brace being slightly uncomfortable as well, she wore it because it did its job. It allowed her to walk for the day. Ankles are hard to put back in and it hurts like hell so she tried not to put herself in the position to have to do that too much. Who can afford to go to the doctor for every dislocation? Doctors 7-15 times a week? Who has that money? She learned to do it herself. It sucked, but she managed.

She managed.

That was a good way to describe her struggle with chronic pain. She managed. Every day. For her family, partner, the reptiles who depended on her, and occasionally, for herself. If manage was all she could do, then manage she would.

Tomorrow.

Tonight was her night to feel her feelings and write it all down.

13. New Year's Day

11:30 at night on New Years Day
I made the choice to leave.
I packed a bag with all I had
So I'd have everything I'd need.
I told you I was leaving,
You weren't keen on believing
That you weren't in control anymore.

When you would scream at me,
I blamed myself.
When something went wrong,
It was always my fault.
I spent so long trying to make you happy,
I forgot about my happy.

I told you I was leaving.
You laughed right in my face.
I told you I was serious.
You said, "Yeah, no way."
I told you I was leaving now
And you made me feel small again.
I wasn't giving up and you knew it.
You started to beg and apologize,
But I wasn't falling for that again.

Now I'm gone.
There's no holding me back.
I am free.
No hands restricting me.
I am fine.
I can be who I was always meant to be.
Because of New Years Day.

New Year's day was a crazy ride.
Death and freedom both ensued.
Any other day it started like,
Until I heard the news.
She was walking home,
He took her life,
Not even calling 911.
They found her in the morgue,
Jane Doe, New Years Day.

He picked me up that night from work,
Started in again.
I told him about the loss of my friend.
I asked please, not tonight.
No fighting or yelling again tonight.
Just for this one night, let me be.
I need to mourn in peace.

He couldn't let me.
He agreed, of course.
But no, he couldn't let me.
As we drove down the road,
He started screaming and I knew.
This was the last New Year's day with him.

At 11:30 I packed my bag,
And told you I was leaving.
You told me I was wrong,
But I did it.
I got away from you, got my life back.
Now it's all that I can do to keep the memories from
surfacing when I see someone like you.
But I've moved on from your abuse.
I finally found my happy.
All because of New Years Day.

14. Creating A Stranger

I always wondered, as a child, why my father never had the love for me that he did for my little brother and sister. I wondered if I did something wrong, if I could do something to win that love, if there was something I was missing. I spent years thinking that my small self was the reason for the emptiness I felt from him.

I often asked myself why I wasn't enough. Why he had to go create a new family when he already had me. What was I supposed to think as a kid? How was I to know that all of the things he didn't do weren't my fault. How was I supposed to believe that he chose not to see me on purpose, of his own volition, of his own choice. How do you tell an eight-year-old that? A nine-year-old? Ten?

How is a child that young supposed to understand that it isn't that they aren't good enough, it is that the parent made a choice. And then another. And another until that long string of choices stretched out over years of concerts and report cards. Until that string of choices led to high school and college graduations, big moves, big events, big dreams being missed completely. How was that kid turned teen supposed to believe that they didn't have to do anything at all to lose him? That he made that decision willingly and then the other family just happened. It is hard to make an adult understand that, but a child?

I always wondered why I wasn't enough, wasn't wanted, was replaced. That's how it felt for so long. I used to make up these big speeches about leaving me behind and not understanding why they got the love that I so desperately wanted. The love that I tried so hard to earn when I was around him. The love I saw reflected toward them instead, every time. This isn't to say I didn't want them to have it. I just wanted some too. Any bit of love or reassurance would do. I was practically begging for it. I helped as much as I could in hopes that his appreciation would turn to love, even slowly. I just wanted what they had. I wanted to see the love in his eyes that they got every day pointed in my direction too. I loved my little siblings and was also so jealous of them and what they had. Who they had. The naïve child in me didn't see what was going on. I didn't know what avoidance was. I didn't know who he was before me. I didn't know that people can truly detach from you and feel bad, but still not fix it. I didn't know that no amount of dishes or help or begging would get me that outward manifestation of love that I was looking for, hoping for. I didn't know until I no longer wanted it.

I hit 10 and another Christmas came and went without so much as a card or a call to wish a happy holiday. That was the year I broke. I didn't understand the why, but the hard facts hit me in the face like a ton of bricks as I sat crying in the lap of the person who had taken his place. I cried and mourned the idea of ever having that love that I had seen him convey. I gave up on the notion of having him back in my life.

Over the next few years, I let myself hope when he would call, hope that maybe this time he would follow through. Maybe he would call again soon. Then I would watch myself fall to pieces again and again when the inevitable came true. I kept doing that to myself for a long time. When I got into my teens, a phone call cut the rest of the cord for me, cut off all the hope I had been letting myself savor and suffer over.
The day I asked adult questions and got berated for it was the day I realized that if he could speak to me that way, he could never love me the way I had hoped. When asking why there is no support, and the first reaction is minimization and defensiveness, why would you expect anyone to have hope for a relationship of any worth to come out of that?
I hung up on the raised voice and the anger and cried, letting out 13 years' worth of loss and grief.

I let myself mourn the father that I had always held a shred of hope for. Then I burned the shred of hope I had left.

I made him into a stranger in my mind, mostly because that is truly what he was. I didn't know anything about him to call him more than that. Can you fathom not knowing who your father is as a person? I saw glimpses during visits of him with the other adults, him with my siblings, him with coworkers, him with his animals. They were all different faces who I rarely remembered and I could see that even they held more of an interest than I did to him. So I stopped trying.

I tried to stop being angry and holding a grudge. It took me years, but I managed to forgive him and myself for holding onto anger and resentment for so long. For trying to hold onto him for too long.

I'm not angry that he isn't in my life anymore because who gets angry about not knowing a stranger?

15. Silence

I filled the silence because I hated the silence. Because it made me uncomfortable. Because I feared it.
Do you know what it is like to fear silence?
It isn't exactly the silence you fear in those moments. It is what the silence can become. What it can bring. What it can mean for you and your safety.

You see, for a while, silence meant a likelihood of pain and degradation. Silence meant that I somehow inherently did something wrong. Silence meant why can't you do this right or why can't you be more like this person. So, I began to fear it for what it could bring. What it could be. Fearing silence as a concept is scary, but when you break down why, it can be fixed. I was so afraid of the silence, and I couldn't figure out why for the longest time.

I'm afraid of silence if I'm afraid of the reactions of the person I'm sharing the silence with. I don't fear silence with my best friend, sitting and scrolling on our phones. I don't fear silence with my family when there is a pause in conversation. But when I am not sure of what kind of reaction I will get from someone, especially if they have reacted in a way that has hurt me before, I fear that silence like it is a beast on my back. I fear it like the jump scares in a scary movie or the mini heart attack you get when you almost fall.

From what I've found, identifying the reason you are scared puts a name to it. And putting a name, a reason, to that fear is part of the battle. Just like accepting you have a problem is the first step to recovery from addiction, accepting that your fear has a name and a reason is the first step to getting rid of that fear. It is the first step in being comfortable in silence again. I am still working on it, every day. Realizing how comfortable in silence I can be when the people around me are kind and respectful, when I know there won't be any random things I did wrong or any unreasonable reactions, is so shocking. In the best way possible of course, but shocking, nonetheless.

As someone who never truly felt comfortable in silence, in fear of what others would do or say, in fear of doing or saying something that would be wrong or annoying, finding that comfort is shocking. Almost jumping in a cold pool on a hot day shocking. Refreshing but not at all properly prepared for how it would feel.

I am learning to find peace in silence. I don't need my world to be so loud to drown it out anymore. I'm not quite as good at silence in my own brain, but in the world around me? I'm getting better.

That's all I can ask of myself, right? Just progress. Practice makes progress. And any progress you make, you should be proud of it. Every stepping stone counts.

Just because it isn't the end of the stones, that doesn't mean the one step didn't get you somewhere.

16. We Are Different. Deal With It.

You want me to do things in a way that is easier for you and me? There isn't one. Things that would make things easier for you make them harder for me. Our brains and bodies work in opposite ways. My brain and body hate doing things the same way every single day. My pathological demand avoidance will make every task seem that much harder just because of the time restraint. No matter how much time I'm given, if you make me orient my schedule to what's easiest for your brain, it is going to make it exponentially more difficult for mine.

You can do the same thing every day without it getting harder to do. You can go off of a minute-by-minute schedule and have it make your day easier. You can focus on that time management because you don't have chronic pain. Because you aren't disabled.

Your way of life is easier because it aligns with the neurotypical world. My way of life is difficult. My way of life has me in agony, a lot. It makes doing things difficult in general, but even more so when my brain interprets it as a "must". It is exponentially harder for me to do things at the same time every day because every day isn't the same for me in life.

I don't wake up in the same mood with no pain and no dysregulation. I wake up different, day to day. Sometimes I wake up with a dislocated ankle and have to put it back in before I can even leave my house. Sometimes I wake up with little pain but end up sore by the time I get to work. Sometimes it is a bad pain day, sometimes it is a good one. Sometimes I don't know what it is until I physically get up out of bed. None of that makes me less than or incapable, but it makes me different. It makes me work and think and act different.

I get that you don't experience those things. I get that. I'm happy for you, really I am. But you not experiencing those things doesn't mean I don't. If something works for you, it doesn't mean it will work for everyone. If it is easy for you, it may be extremely difficult for someone else. You and other people don't get to decide what is easy or hard for others. What will work for others. You have to ask if you want to know. You have to take the initiative to find out why things are done the way they are.

You have to accept that everyone isn't like you. You have to accept that everyone isn't you.

Every single person on this earth thinks and acts differently. Everyone has different struggles and different things that are easy for them. You don't get to decide what works for other people. You get to decide what works for you and what you want to ask for. But there will come a point where your unrealistic expectations bite you in the ass. Especially when you are putting them on someone else.

17. Recovering From Abuse

Recovering from abuse is hard.

It is hard to not believe that you deserved it. It is hard to get their voice out of your head. To not need to change the station when a song you once loved is now nothing more than a painful memory.

It is hard to not carry that forward with you, all the things you were told were wrong when you were really just being controlled. Being controlled by him because that's what made him feel in control of his life. Controlled by him because that was what he grew up being. Controlled by him because you didn't know how not to be. You didn't know how to leave him when he had convinced you it was your fault in the first place. Your fault that he yelled, your fault that he screamed, your fault that everything you did wasn't good enough and everything you tried to do was useless.

He convinced you that you as a person had no worth, though you had felt worthless before meeting him. You often wondered if that's part of the reason you fell for his trap. Because he made you feel worth something, then pulled that rug out from underneath you and turned into

the devil that the disguise had been hiding. He ripped off
the tearaway personality and became the monster your
parents always told you wasn't hiding under your bed.

They were right. The monster was never under your bed.
He was waiting to meet you at your most vulnerable and
convince you he was exactly what you needed. He did
and said all the things you had always wanted someone
to do and say to you. He was kind and patient,
introducing you to music and other things you had never
experienced. He had some differences and flaws, but
nothing that ever seemed dangerous or insurmountable.

You were blissfully happy, not realizing that he had you
right where he wanted you. He wanted you to be so
distracted and in love with who you thought he was that
when he ripped that mask off and started treating you
the way he always intended to, you wouldn't be as quick
to leave. You aren't as quick to leave because he's been so
great up until now. He has been kind, but now that
kindness was ripped away and there is ice where that
warmth used to be.

When he starts changing and you start worrying, he gets
defensive. He tells you that it is your fault that he gets so
angry. If you would just do what he asked, he wouldn't
be angry. So you try to follow directions exactly, but

even when you do, he is angry for some other reason. Slowly, everything you used to do that he would be proud of you for and help you with, that all turns into things you can't do right and reasons you can do it yourself.

You try your best to not make him angry, to not add to the anger he seems to carry like an extra limb. But no matter how hard you try, you can never do it right. You can never say the right thing, do the right thing, make the right decisions. Everything you attempt gets ridiculed, every thought you have is immediately discarded. Every ask for help is met with a scoff and an excuse as to why you are on your own again. But when you don't want to help him or his family, the anger comes back. Always unbalanced expectations, always your fault.

But it isn't. It isn't your fault. That is what he told you so that you would lose faith in yourself. He told you that you were useless enough times that you started to believe it. He told you that no one else would love you if you left him and you believed him. He made sure to grind you into the dirt enough times for you to lose the will to get up, to go anywhere else, to escape.

He wore you down until you were a shell of a person.

Until every time he touched you felt like acid hitting your skin and every time you looked in the mirror, you felt disgusted at what you saw. You saw his thoughts reflected in your skin, seeing all his comments as if they were written on the parts of you he said were so wrong. You hated that you couldn't separate his comments from your skin and it made you want to scrub off every layer of skin you had until there was nothing else for you to see those words in.

It isn't just words, but his actions that hurt you. The shoves when you are in the way, the thumb-sized bruises you explain away to the people you can't bear to tell, the nights when he violates you, the times when he is so angry at you that you aren't allowed to sleep in bed with him. You have to sleep at the end of the bed like the family dog or on the floor with a single sheet. Or on the unpadded wooden top bunk of the bed, the strips of wood pressing into your skin so you can't get comfortable.

It is the violence you see and hear from him when you get in the way of his games. You walk quickly in front of the screen while his game is going and he acts like you just shot him. He screams and calls you names and tells you that you should know better. That you shouldn't be interrupting the thing that he loves. That he doesn't want to see you when he is playing games and that you now have to leave the room completely because now you've pissed him off.

It's the fear of what will happen when you inevitably do something wrong or say something wrong. It is the constant anxiety of when the next unreasonable burst of anger will happen and ruin everyone's day. It is the hatred for yourself when someone's comments and opinions have taken over your own. When you have been stripped of personality, free will, autonomy, the willingness to live. When you would rather take your own life than live another day with him.

It isn't that you don't try. You do. Sitting in the same closet you always hide and cry in, holding onto the gun he doesn't know you have, staring down the barrel, willing yourself to be done. You raise the determination to put it to your head. Tight to your temple with your finger on the trigger. Inches from the cold, quiet nothingness you long for. The escape from this hellscape you've fallen into.

You sit there, gun pressed to your head, mind racing, tears flowing down your face. Then you lower the gun to your lap and you cry harder. You feel more ashamed of yourself for not being able to end it. For not being able to put your family through the pain you know it would cause. You can't bear the possibility that you live through it somehow. That he is the last thing you would see.

So you can't do it. You cry and put the gun back in the case, hiding it in the back of the closet, away from his sight. You live another day, and another. Not because you want to, but because you've always been told there is no better option.

Leaving abuse is hard, but healing from abuse is harder. It takes so long and so much work. It takes almost constant effort and setbacks. It takes perseverance. And it sucks. You won't like it, in fact, you'll hate it sometimes. You'll ask yourself why you are the one doing the work when he messed you up. You'll ask the universe why this had to happen to you, why you couldn't make yourself leave sooner, why you can't heal faster.

You will bring toxicity with you into new situations and you will have to relearn how to interact with others. You will have to reset your fight or flight response, which is horribly difficult to do. You will have to learn to set boundaries and, more importantly, how to stand up for yourself when they are crossed. You'll have to learn to trust your gut and your opinions instead of depending

on those around you to tell you who you are. You have
to relearn how to think for yourself, regulate your
emotions, trust people and yourself again.

Leaving and healing from abuse is like coming out of a
multi-year coma. You have to relearn life. How to walk
to your own rhythm, talk to yourself kindly and to
others respectfully, breathe through anxiety attacks and
crying fits, how to say no to things you don't want.

Learning how to be human again is one of the hardest
things you'll ever have to do. It is also one of the most
important things you'll have to do.

It is rough and you will want to give up sometimes.
Some people do. Some people lose their battle along the
way. If you don't give up, you've got a battle ahead of
you that will take years. It won't always seem worth it
and it will seem like you are moving backwards at
times.

Recovering from abuse is hard.
Relearning who you are is hard.
Realizing that you stopped being a person for the sake of
someone who never wanted the best for you is terrible.

Some people will act like it should be easy, that you are

being dramatic or over-emotional about "nothing". Those people don't get what is happening and of course they don't. They just know what you tell them, if they even believe you. He convinced you they wouldn't so you don't even feel like you should try.

You are a warrior.

No matter what part of this process you are in or have been in, you are a warrior.

No matter what part of this process you are in, I am proud of you for keeping yourself alive.
If you lose this battle, I'm proud of you for having tried.

Either way, he is wrong. That person is wrong. You are not worthless or useless or stupid. You aren't a waste of space, a nothing, a bother or an annoyance. You aren't any of the things he said. You aren't a horrible person, you aren't wrong for being who you are. He convinced you of those things knowing he was wrong. He convinced you of those things so you were easier to keep, to control. It isn't your fault that you fell into that trap. It is designed to catch you. It is built specifically to put you into a fake sense of safety and confidence, then drop you through a trap door into the nine circles of hell.

Recovering from abuse is hard.

Progress isn't fast and can seem to go on forever.

But your milestones will come.

Someday you will reset those cycles.

You will be able to walk in front of a TV while it is on without fearing the outcome.

You'll be able to ask for what you need and know that need will be met.

You'll believe that you can not only do some things right, but most things.

Yes, setbacks will happen.

They will be painful and make you feel ashamed and make you question if you have even made any progress at all.

You have.

You have made so much progress and I am so proud of you. I am proud of the person you are and the person you are evolving into. I am proud of your efforts and the little wins along the way. I am proud of you for trying, most of all.

You are progress.

You are improving.

You are healing.

You are worth everything.
I am proud of you.
Keep going.

18. The Lessons Reptiles Can Teach

Reptiles are amazing creatures that are capable of so much more than what humans give them credit for. They are intelligent, curious, adventurous, hilarious creatures. They have amazing personalities. And for not being able to speak English, they communicate very clearly and they will stand up for themselves when they feel threatened. Reptiles are so misunderstood, even in some modern care guides. People have very real fear and ignorance around reptiles and it is totally misguided. If you treat them with respect and learn to read their body language, reptiles are just as amazing to care for as dogs and cats. I believe they are the ideal animal to have, if you are ready for research.

In the many years I've had reptiles and with the different reptiles I've fostered, they are still so interesting and surprising every day. They teach me new things all the time.

They have reminded me that patience and calmness are the key to a terrified creature. They teach me about their limits, and sometimes my own. They show me what true trust is when they go from feral to cuddles. They show me what forgiveness is whenever I have to mess with stuck shed or trim nails and they go back to letting me pet them after.

They teach me about the importance of having your environment serve you. If they don't have the correct lights, vitamins, and food, they suffer. We can learn at least that from them. Your environment should serve you; not what others want it to be. If the lizard comes from the desert, that needs to be replicated in their heat and humidity levels. If they were plucked from the Savannah desert, they would need higher humidity levels than other species. If that species eats insects in the wild, don't feed it mice in captivity.

Reptiles teach me that being patient with a creature who is scared is all you really need to do to gain its trust. I work with frightened, neglected, rescued animals and the fact that I get to spend every day earning their trust and showing them that all humans aren't trash is truly one of the reasons I get out of bed in the morning. The fact that my reptiles exist has been the single reason I've risen from my bed for the day, even if I slunk back into it later. They make my world go round. They can teach us so much. I've learned so many important lessons and had plenty of chances to practice my patience since this journey began.

I've realized recently that seeing the animal that came to me terrified and neglected blossom into a fully healthy, full-of-personality lizard is one of the main purposes of my life. Helping to heal the animals that have been harmed by other humans is a mission that I know a lot of people share. It is one I take personally. I've seen animals come in that are in the worst condition, not only physically but psychologically. The way they stay close to the ground, hide most of the time they are awake, sleep completely hidden, move very quickly and fidgety, react to any and all sounds, and hyperventilate just because you looked at them makes my heart break. It also makes me angry. Angry for what these creatures have suffered for no good reason. Angry at the owners who just took the pet shop's word for it and didn't do any more research than that. Angry with the people unnecessarily breeding reptiles and other animals while every shelter is bursting at the seams with homeless pets that already exist. Angry with the people who throw reptiles away like trash, sometimes in the same manner.

But seeing that same terrified animal grow to trust you, even to the point of coming to you for food or attention, is so rewarding. It helps you almost as much as it helps them. By showing them that you are safe and trustworthy, and you will have the patience they will undoubtedly need, you show yourself the same things. You show yourself what you are capable of when you show them your kindness and your love. They deserve that, like you do. Seeing an animal grow to trust you can be the thing you need to show yourself.

I care for reptiles because they allow me to. Because they watch my movements and my behaviors and my kindness toward them and they find me worthy of the beginnings of trust. As I stay consistent with those qualities, they gain more trust for me as time goes on until they no longer fear any action I may take. They don't hyperventilate when I look at them or run from me when I try to pick them up. They don't try to bite me when I have to mess with their toes, and they don't charge me the second I look away. They give back the same patience they were given. They return it in the form of trust and willingness to tolerate the things they would've feared from me before. Earning the trust of any animal is rewarding, but when it is a reptile, there is something different about the level of trust you are given. Unexplainably but definitely different. It is something I love. And the fact that what I do makes them able to not only be removed from bad situations but also put into the best situations possible for them after me makes every worry and scratch and tear worth it.

Many people have asked me how I foster without keeping every animal I get.

For me, it is because I started young. I started fostering feral kittens when I was in my single digit years. I graduated from feral kittens to feral cats. Then I went out into the big wide world and got into reptiles. I rescued my first reptile when I really needed to be rescued myself. He was my saving grace and my reason for living at a time when I didn't have many others. I was eventually rescued, but I couldn't save him and me. It was a choice that I did not, and never will, take lightly. When I got the chance to rescue another lizard of the same kind, I didn't hesitate. He has been the light of my life for the last 8 years and I wouldn't give him up for anything. Learning about his species and other species like him, I eventually rescued a couple more reptiles of my own.

Then I was sent a fostering link for a reptile rescue, and I was hooked. I got my first foster, and he was in rough shape, but so sweet. Even through everything he had experienced, he was so kind and grateful. That sealed the deal for me. I won't say it doesn't have its challenges and sacrifices. But I wouldn't give them up or change it. I love being the temporary, healing home that acts as a steppingstone on their way to their perfect place. I am grateful for being able to be that guide, that helping hand that they don't want but do need. And although they can't say the words 'thank you', I've seen the gratitude in those tiny eyes. I've noticed their movements become smooth and unbothered. I've seen them not react to a sound that scared them so badly they hid before. I've seen the change I can help create. It is worth every minute I spend on them and every bug I wrangle and every courageous step their little selves take. They are worth it. They will never not be worth it.

19. Learning to Un-Trauma a Brain

She knew it was confusing for him. Why she apologized about everything and always thought his anger was her fault. Why she flinched with no provocation or refused when he offered to buy her anything or pay for anything. She knew that he didn't understand. She was both grateful and not. She was grateful for him to have never experienced the trauma it takes to turn your brain into a backwards winding clock. She was glad he didn't have that experience, but she did wish he understood sometimes.

She wanted to scream sometimes with the memories, but she didn't want him to have those images in his head too. Those words.

She wished he understood sometimes though. Like when she apologized for the thousandth time that day and she felt like digging herself into a hole and never coming out because she knows how much that can annoy some people. She wanted to disappear in those moments.

But for him to understand all of that would mean that she would have to tell him.

Tell him about the horrible things that were said and done to her. Things that were said as if she wasn't in the room. Things she was made to do for making someone angry. The humanity that felt as if it were stripped away a little more every time he screamed at her or gave her a look of disgust as he walked away.

She would have to tell him about the times she sat in the closet, wishing that this wasn't her life but being too controlled and feeling too helpless to do anything about it. She would have to tell him how much she hurt and how tired she was when she was forced out of bed again to do someone else's work who was more in pain than her, when pain wasn't the reason that she was up instead of them.

She would have to tell him about sleeping at the foot of the bed, on the floor, on a wooden top bunk, and worse, with him. She would have to tell him that the smell of a redemption center still gives her a feeling of dread and that every time she smells a bag of bottles at work, she has to stop and steady herself.

She would have to tell him why there are places she won't go and people she will no longer speak to because she knows where that information might go.

She would have to tell him that she looked over her shoulder for years after she left for fear of him being around the next corner. She would have to tell him about the rose shaped napkin in the menu holder at a job she had left just a week before that drained the blood from her face like she had seen a ghost. She would have to tell him that every time she sees a truck like his, she wants to disappear and also crash it. She would have to tell him about the day she left and how difficult and freeing it was at the same time.

She would have to tell him all of these things because how else would he understand why she apologizes so much? It seems random and intense, but is it? Or is it just a sign that someone once fucked that person up so badly that they now apologize for existing? They apologize just for taking up space. For just being a person on earth.

How do you help someone understand why you are apologizing so much without explaining the story of how you got there? How do you answer that question, truly answer it, without traumatizing the person on the other end? If they consent to the secondhand trauma, does that make it better? Does it make it better for them after you've shared something that not only rocks their worldview and floods them with emotions and questions, but also changes their perspective of you, even if they don't notice it? How are you supposed to help them understand if understanding means handing off trauma?

Does she just give that trauma out like a gift? No, of course not, because it sucks. She doesn't want it and she definitely doesn't want to make someone else carry around a duplicate copy with them forever. So how does she make him understand why she has the urge to apologize for everyday things?

When she apologizes for doing something inconsequential, should she explain why? Should she tell him that she used to get berated when she did that, so now she feels immense guilt and fear and the immediate need to apologize whenever it happens because sometimes the apologies were the only thing to keep the screaming at bay. The guilt and fear were deeply instilled in her over time. She felt guilty for making too much noise when doing house chores, taking too long in the bathroom, standing in the way of what someone needs. But she was never actually too loud or taking too long. She just felt that way because she was told that she was useless every time she wasn't immediately moving out of the way, even if she didn't know which way the person needed to go. She felt it when she dropped a fork in the sink and it made a sound with anyone else within earshot. She feels it when someone's facial expression changes into that of anger or disgust, even if not toward her.

She would have to tell him all this. He would have to hear it and take that into his brain.
If he was willing, maybe. If he asked, she would tell him. If he really wanted to know, she would recount the events, the ones she could remember. But that meant reliving them. She did that anyway for her writing, but reliving and relaying them to someone who cares for you so deeply... Someone that you know will picture how you suffered and will want to love you through it... She would do it if he asked, but how?

How do you tell someone about a life you once lived where he never would have recognized you, the shell of a person you were then. How would you explain that you were a victim then, and a survivor now. That you have all of this in your mind, but you have to just keep going? How would she tell him all the sorrows and traumas of her past life? She was still surviving some of the monsters in her head.

How would she explain that her being afraid when he is angry is not a reflection on him or their relationship?

How would she explain that her traumatized nervous system and fucked up fight or flight response don't control her conscious brain, that she knows he isn't dangerous, she knows he won't get violent, she knows he won't scream or degrade her, but that fear is still there.

Nothing that he can do is going to make her think he will do any of that. But the fear is still there. The fear is what she works on, day in and day out. Fear is one of the things she is still surviving.
She works every day to retrain her nervous system and her responses to what is <u>actually</u> dangerous vs what is a bagel that you must return. She has to teach her brain that not everything is loud and painful. Not every chance you take or person you talk to is going to treat you like some people have.

How does she explain that all to him? To anyone? How do you tell someone that you are constantly shedding the trauma of the past, but that it takes years. It isn't just years of time passing. That shit is work. Hard work. Unlearning trauma is hard. She thought she knew that when she started her journey. Boy was she wrong. She was correct in how hard, but she never expected what it would take to feel like a person again.

How would she explain to him that, in all the ways he had helped her, his reassurance that she deserved life and happiness was one of the most helpful things he did?

Unlearning trauma is hard.

Trying to explain your past to someone that doesn't deserve the trauma is hard; hell, even just the decision is hard.

Fuck it. Do it anyway. You deserve to be and feel like a human again. You deserve that always.

20. Our Stories Unfold

We love and lose. We hate and then gain a new understanding. One we never thought we would have. When we learn things we never thought we would learn, it brings a new meaning to life. One we never thought possible. It broadens our horizons and makes us realize things we never thought about knowing. When this happens, we never expect it, but need to hold it tight and not let go. Hold not only the experience, but also the knowledge that was brought to light by this experience.

I was caught in the wake of an inner storm, time and time again. I thought that all I could do was hold on and brace for impact. So that is what I did. And in came impact. It knocked me down, but not out. Knocking me out will take a harder hit than anything I have received thus far. One day, that hit may come. But the one thing I can't allow myself to do is sit around and wait for it. I can't allow myself to act as though that final, mind-numbing blow has already happened. Because it hasn't. That is what I can't do.

Yes, I struggle. Every day of my damn life.

Yes, I hurt. Also every day of my damn life. But I learn

something new every day as well. Sometimes, it is how to hold my tongue better. Sometimes, I learn a new fact about someone I know. And sometimes, I learn what my new breaking point is.

Yes, I am broken, but I get up every day. And every day, I hope that the thing I learn today is how to mend what is broken in me. That isn't usually what I learn.

I am still standing. And that, in itself, is worth another day above ground, searching for the next day's lesson. The next lesson could be futile or sad. Not all lessons are fun or happy or useful. But they all matter. They are all necessary. And, as much as it seems like they are not sometimes, they are all important. Each day you live is a milestone. Each step you take is an adventure. And each moment you live turns into a moment in time that you can never take back and never forget.

Time doesn't stop for anyone. Even if sometimes, it feels like it does. Even when you wish it would. I used to wish everyday for a miracle. Every moment in time was spent hoping that better things would come along. Miracles are made, not happened upon. Things that happen sometimes seem crazy. They seem unbelievable and lovely and unfathomable.

Sometimes, miracles are strange. They take the place of regular thoughts and fill our minds with hope, like the fairytales of our younger years. There are reasons those fairytales don't exist. People never made them to be real. When you think about your childhood fairytales, do you think of the story and the characters? Is that what you think of? Or do you immediately recall the nights lying in bed, trying not to fall asleep while the person you look up to most is telling you wonderful stories of happiness, adventures, and ever-afters?

Which one induces those childish grins and giggles, even when you have grown old enough to know that those places and characters and adventures don't exist? You still feel the excitement and the rush because it wasn't the characters and castles and adventures that made those stories memorable. It was the feelings and emotions that the hope in those stories invoked.

The feeling when the phrase "And they lived happily ever after" was uttered. The smile when you imagined the eternal joy of those characters. The feeling of excitement when asking for just 'one more story', knowing that you probably wouldn't get it that night. The feeling of contentment as you drifted off to sleep, dreaming of forever and ever, love, happiness, and the ability to dream.

Those moments, however few there were, are the reasons you smile when someone mentions your favorite fairytale or even the song you couldn't wait for someone to sing before you could sleep. The tiny details of the journeys of our lives aren't what keep us smiling. The memories they invoke are. That tiny smile when you hear "one upon a time" or the laugh you let out when someone reminds you of a prank you once pulled.

The stories caused the emotions. The emotions are what we see and feel for the rest of our lives. In some ways, the moments of our lives are like those childhood stories of old.

We saw the stories unfold. Some were good; some were bad. All were important. All invoked emotions and some of those emotions stay with us.

Forever and ever, until the end of time.

21. I Like Me

There was a time in my life when I really and truly never thought I could like who I was. I couldn't possibly imagine looking in a mirror and liking what I saw. I couldn't imagine not wanting to crawl out of my skin at every glance, every comment that my brain just couldn't agree with, the things it couldn't see.

But I like myself. Not every little bit of me, which is what I thought was required before. I don't have to like those things to like me. I am not those tiny things that are the only clouds in my near blue sky. I am me. I encompass all of myself and I am not defined by those little things. I am not defined by anything but what I define myself as. No one gets to make that choice for me anymore.

The funny thing is, the more I like and respect myself as a person, the more I see my past-self reflected in others. Now that I am cognizant of being non-judgmental, kind, and genuinely aware of my impact on others, I can see even clearer who doesn't share those traits. Who hasn't healed in those ways yet. Who doesn't care who they hurt.

I work every day to not be that person again. I dislike

who I used to be. Not for how I looked, but for who I was. Who I forced myself to be to try to fit in. To try to assimilate. I hate that I let myself hide me because of others' criticisms. I hate that I silenced myself so others could speak. I hate that part of me still wants to do that, wants to shrink into the corner in confrontations. I hate that that was who I was.

But I love me for working out of that. I love me for standing up and using my voice once again. I'm proud of me for learning to advocate for myself and continuing to try even when I struggle and fail at it in some moments. I'm proud of me for being able to say that I'm proud of me and say it honestly. I've never been able to do that before now.

Yes, I've been proud of things I've done, but not of me. Not of who I am as a person. I am proud of me for my accomplishments and my steps taken. I'm proud of my progress and my realization that there will never be perfect. Practice makes progress, and progress should always be celebrated. I'm proud of me for knowing who I am finally, and I am willing to stand up for her. I buried who I was when I was young for the sake of everyone's comfort. I will never do that again. I deserve to be who I am and be proud of me. I have done a lot of work to find me again. The me I can be proud of and be excited to show others without shame. At 30 years old, being able to say that I am proud of who I am is probably the best gift I could give myself.

I am proud of my accomplishments, what I do for others, what I do for my foster animals, and what I am finally doing for myself. I'm going to stand up for that girl from now on. I may fail at times, and it may mean that some people are no longer in my life if they don't fit, but that is the price I am willing and proud to pay to stay being me.

I will no longer surrender myself to others' will, stifle myself so others can thrive, quiet myself so others aren't bothered, or be timid and stoop so others can step over me. If an obstacle is what that makes me, then an obstacle I shall become. But I will no longer be a doormat, bending to others' will, surrendering and burying who I am to appease someone else.

I will continue being me until I have come to an end.
Until then, I like me.
And I'm keeping her.